Steering Through It

Navigating Life-Threatening Illness...
Acceptance, Survival And Healing

Lynn McLaughlin

ISBN 978-1-7750017-0-6

Front Cover Artwork: Sari Richter
Back Cover – Author Image: Rob Moroz

For information: www.steeringthroughit.com

First edition
Published and printed in Canada

Library and Archives Canada registration, book layout and production management through the TRI Publishing™ program
TRIMATRIX Management Consulting Inc.
www.trimatrixmanagement.com

Steering Through It

This book is dedicated to Ken, Shayne, Marina and Mitch, without whom I could not have stemmed the tide.

Contents

Introduction

I had no idea what the future held — whether I would be alive for one more day, or for even another hour. At that moment, the clock stopped. It was Saturday, July 13th, 2013. That was the day I began journaling. My boat had started to rock, and I could not see a clear course forward through the oncoming storm.

A life-threatening illness crushes the world around you, and around those you love. How do we all cope with the diagnosis physically, emotionally, and spiritually? How do we move on? What are the most helpful ways to support others in crisis? In the end, what does it all mean?

I have written this memoir with the hope that my story will help to minimize the impact of such "surprises" that might be thrown at you and your family — surprises that the medical profession cannot prepare you for. Whether you are on your own journey to recovery, or whether you are a spouse, a parent, a sibling, a child, a friend, a partner, an uncle or aunt, a niece, nephew, or an in-law of someone with a life-threatening diagnosis, it is my hope that this book will move you to believe that your actions and positive mindset have the power to drive acceptance, survival, and healing.

Chapter One
The Detour

Saturday, 13 July

The incessant noise in this cramped space is nauseating... a repetitive shrill followed by the roar of a motorcycle revving its engine. The pounding of a sledgehammer, a screeching emergency siren, a dull hum. Silence. I lie here clutching the panic button.

Immediately following the MRI at Windsor Regional Hospital, I was directed to the emergency department. My headaches had been getting worse and I had tinnitus in my left ear, but I had shrugged it off. I attributed the symptoms to turning 50, and the increased responsibility of being promoted to a supervisory role at work. I'd already seen an audiologist and an optometrist, but those consultations had yielded no clues as to the cause of my headaches.

Now, alone and waiting to be called into the emergency department, my mind whirled with the possibilities. The reception area held approximately 20 chairs arranged in rows. The gentleman sitting beside me was reading the local newspaper. After a 10-minute wait that felt like an eternity, a nurse led me into a curtained cubicle. On either side, I could hear medical practitioners gathering personal health information from other patients and explaining their diagnoses. Clearly, whatever I was about to be advised would not be said in privacy. The apprehension intensified.

A woman whom I guessed to be about my age stood outside of my cubicle. She was dressed in a medical gown and wore her dark hair pulled back. She was reading a chart. Was it mine? Her face was blank. She pushed the curtain aside as she entered the cubicle. I sat on the hospital bed, facing her. She flipped through several pages and then introduced herself. Without hesitation, she rattled off my diagnosis. Her words fell like fragments.

"I'm sorry to inform you ... an abnormal lesion ... aggressive ..."

A brain tumour. A brain tumour the size of a golf ball, growing in my left temporal lobe.

I stopped breathing. I stared in disbelief at the physician as she spoke. I felt my heart palpitating and I began to sweat, but part of me remained detached from everything. Smiling automatically, I repeated her words. I was at risk of a stroke, seizure, or coma. It was a ticking time bomb. My frozen expression masked emotions that I could not name.

The edema — that is, the swelling — was so extensive that it had caused my brain to shift more than a centimetre to the right. Within minutes, I was prescribed steroids and anti-seizure medications. Blood work was done, and my temperature and blood pressure were taken. I was given an urgent referral to a neurosurgery clinic for a full consultation. My appointment was in five days.

Everything in my life had changed forever. I had no idea what the future held, or even if I would survive the next week. How would I cope emotionally, spiritually, and physically? How could I tell my family the news? How does a mother inform three teenaged children that she has a life-threatening diagnosis? How could my aging father support his daughter through such a thing?

I left the emergency department and bolted to my car. Before going to the hospital, I had dropped off my daughter and her friend at the shopping mall. I could not pick them up. I could not face anyone. Fumbling with my cell phone, I called my husband. He is a police officer, and he had worked the night shift. It was now mid-afternoon, and he would be just waking up.

"Hi, Ken. Are the boys around?" I asked. "I need to speak with you privately."

He asked what was wrong. I blurted it out. There was dead silence on the other end of the line. I hastily told him the rest. "They don't know if it's cancer, but I need surgery. We'll get through this." He asked if I was alright to drive. "Yes," I said. He arranged for the girls to get a ride home from the mall. I still have no idea how I got home that day, given my state of mind.

After much discussion, we decided to wait until we had all details before telling anyone, even our children. We had far too many questions ourselves. What was a craniotomy? Was the tumour cancerous? Would I need radiation or chemotherapy?

Ken had been my best friend since our first date almost 30 years prior, on my twenty-first birthday. Back then, we were both training as officer candidates in Esquimalt, British Columbia, and we have been together since. His strength kept us both going as we laboured through the next few days. I started taking Prednisone to shrink the edema around the tumour, and the medication played havoc with my body and mind. Sleep came haphazardly for no more than four hours per night. While my family slept, I researched and documented my condition. I was determined to acquire more information than the doctor had provided. I was consumed by the need to know. The more we understood, the better prepared we would be.

This was my life, my very essence. "Could it be ending?" I wondered. "Will my kids lose their mother? If I survive, will

I be capable of caring for my family, or even enjoying life in any capacity?" I was determined not to allow myself to become a burden to them.

Monday, 15 July

Why has this road block been thrown up before me? I have always believed that events in our lives occur for a reason. Is this a divine punishment because of the choices I have made in my life? Have I been too self-absorbed? Have I confused my priorities and taken a path not meant for me? Have I not been there for my family and others, as I have always vowed to be? What is there to learn? One thing is for certain: without warning, my life is taking an unexpected and extreme detour. I pray I have not reached a dead end.

I felt an urgency to figure out what I believed — what guided me and held me true to myself. I had been raised Catholic, but had stopped going to church five years before. Although I still believed in most of the church's teachings, I felt strongly that any individual, including a woman, should have the right to serve as a priest. Although we had baptized all three of our children, it wasn't because we believed they needed forgiveness for sins they had committed prior to the time they reached three months of age. Baptism was a family tradition that we decided to honour. For these reasons, I felt a sense of hypocrisy when attending mass, especially when reciting Apostles' Creed: "I believe in the Catholic Church … and life everlasting." I persevered with church for my children's sake. I wanted them to have a strong foundation that would guide them in finding their own faith. I had no regrets when I stepped away, and I have none to this day.

In contrast to my traditional Catholic upbringing, my mother-in-law welcomed any religious or spiritual experience without judgement. She believed in the healing touch, and in the psychic connection. "Each of us has a purpose in this life," she would say. Faced with death, I considered my own spirituality. I pondered whether I had been truly living, or simply existing in this physical realm. What was my purpose? Could I express my deepest values, including the immortality of my soul? What was my inner voice telling me? I would continue to ask myself these questions, and many more, in my quest to understand what was happening to me.

Wednesday, 17 July

How do I protect the people I love from worry? I pledge to remain positive and believe that I will prevail. I will do my best to remember that my mindset has a direct influence on my body. I must shield myself and my family from negativity and fear.

On Thursday, we met with Dr. Morassutti, the neurosurgeon at Windsor Regional Hospital who would be trusted with my life. He had a confident and calm manner, and I trusted him immediately after he introduced himself. He walked us through everything we needed to know, as hard as it was to hear. As we viewed the distressing MRI images, I grew nauseated. They seemed to magnify themselves and jump off the screen.

"It may very well be a meningioma," he said, "and if so, there's a greater than 95 percent chance that it's not cancerous." He looked me right in the eyes. "If we had discovered this sooner, you may have had other options. It is too large now. You have no option but to have an urgent craniotomy."

My mind raced as he listed the risks. My personality, cognition, and motor skills were in jeopardy, and there was a chance that I would regain consciousness without speech. I could die of excessive blood loss. My surgery would be in less than three weeks, which would give the steroids time to shrink the swelling. It all made horrible sense. The short-term memory issues, tinnitus, fatigue — it had been a brain tumour all along.

I needed a moment alone.

⸻

There are no words to articulate how heart-breaking it was to tell our children, Shayne (19), Marina (15), and Mitch (14). We were intent on sharing facts, but only to the extent that was necessary. It felt as though the living room was closing in on us as we spoke to them, each seated on couches, focused on us, expressionless. We had expected some type of emotional response, but they simply asked a few questions. They had clearly sensed something was wrong. In that moment, I was more worried for them than I was for myself.

We contemplated a delay in telling our McLaughlin and Prior families, but knew that we could not put it off for long. There were too many signs that things were not normal. I dreaded the conversations with my father and my two sisters, but especially with my brother, who had suffered the tragic loss of his first fiancé in a car accident nineteen years earlier.

I began by making phone calls to my two younger sisters, Heather and Colleen. We spoke often, so I hoped that asking to drop by for a visit would be welcomed as perfectly normal. Heather, who is a nurse practitioner, heard something in my voice — but I wanted her to be my sister, not a medical consultant.

As Heather later recalled about our conversation that day:

There are just certain times in your life you can never forget! It was a Monday. I was at my hairdresser's, with colour in my hair when my phone rang. "Hi, Heather. What are you up to today? Are you working?" I said I was just at the hairdressers and asked, "What's up?" She replied, "Just thought I would drop by to talk to you about something. Will you be home this afternoon?" I told her I'd be home around 5 p.m.

After we spoke, I felt a sudden ache, a fear. Call it a sister's instinct, but I knew something was wrong. I just knew it. But what was it? I felt the anxiety building as I considered all the possibilities. By 1 p.m., I knew I had to call her back. I felt sick. I sensed something was dreadfully wrong.

"We can talk when I get there," she said.

"No, I have to know," I insisted. I remember begging for some little hint of what it could be. "Well," Lynn said, "I...I have a brain tumour."

Silence, pain, fear, hands trembling, everything closing in. What was I hearing? Was this really happening? 5 p.m. was an eternity away. Having the medical knowledge I do only added to my fear. "Be rational," I thought. "I have to be positive. Statistically, a large percentage of brain tumours are benign. Oh my God! Please don't let this be happening." I felt weak with fear, and I was nauseated. She was alone in the ER when she got the news! How can that happen? Why wasn't I there? Why did she not call? How can she be so strong in the face of everything?

As I was looking at the MRI report after Lynn and Ken arrived, I remember thinking, "Oh my God, could she be in that 10 percent? Less than 10 percent of meningiomas are cancerous. But the tumour is big. How is my sister sitting there so calm? Describing only subtle symptoms sipping on a glass of wine. She is my strength. Strength is running off her." I knew one thing for sure: in God's faith we would find the strength to support her and get through this.

My timing was very poor when I called my sister Colleen. She was at work and didn't answer the phone at first, but within seconds she called me back, asking what was wrong. Her voice was shaky on the phone. She was persistent. Putting off the news would have only caused her to wonder.

Ken and I went to see my father together. Dad, now 73 years old, and my stepmother Carol, are Florida residents but they spend the summer months in Ontario. Dad sat on the couch with Carol beside him. She offered us a drink, as she did on every visit. I declined. I'm sure my anxiety was apparent. I clutched my hands in front of me and shared the news.

Dad was very good at masking his concern, but I noticed that he was chewing the fingernails on his left hand. I could feel the tension in his shoulders as he hugged me. They asked a few questions and we answered honestly, playing a supportive role. I can imagine the conversation between them as they followed us to my brother's home.

Mike and my sister-in-law responded in the same way, assuring us that they would do anything we needed over the coming weeks. Dad offered to call my two half-brothers, Sean and Colin, our family in Michigan.

I would love to have been a fly on the wall after we left each family member's home. I'm sure that's when true emotions and feelings were revealed. I knew that I would never be privy to them. I wondered how I could lessen their worry as the days and nights passed.

My family has always been my rock, and each of them played a role in keeping me on an even keel. If you're on your own journey towards recovery, don't be afraid to lean on your family and friends. Even during times of uncertainty along the way, it is important to remember that you can depend on the love and support of your crew!

My boss needed to be told in person. I felt a very real sense of guilt about the situation, since he and two other members of the senior team were about to retire. This would put additional pressure on him and his exit plan.

Warren was always in the office long before anyone else arrived. I knocked on the open door and asked to speak with him privately. "Do you have any plans for the summer?" he asked as he closed the door behind me.

"My plans have changed," I blurted out.

He was taken aback, but he was very considerate. He understood that my leave of absence had to begin immediately, and agreed to keep the news confidential until I contacted him again later in the week. Afterwards, back in my office, I began to prepare for a turnover — but when and to whom, I had no idea.

Thursday, 18 July

This is exhausting and I just can't find any more words. I will need to find a way to tell my closest friends, but I just can't do it today. My energy now needs to focus on what is before me.

Chapter Two
Giving Up The Helm

In retrospect, I displayed initial symptoms two years prior to the diagnosis. I explained them away, telling myself "it's the new job" or "it's turning 50," when I should have gone to see my physician. I did consult with an audiologist about the tinnitus in my left ear, and about my dizzy spells, which I had attributed to vertigo. When I started to suffer from headaches on a regular basis, Advil was the answer. I eventually conferred with my optometrist, who found no specific cause. Ignoring his advice to make an appointment with my physician, I carried on. One day at work, my headache and nausea were so extreme that I called my brother, who lived close by. No one was at his home at the time, but he gave me the access code to his house. I took medication and slept on his couch until the symptoms passed. I was using denial as a defense mechanism, because I could not face the clear signs that something was terribly wrong with my health.

Waking up every morning with intense headaches is what finally forced my hand. The fatigue was so extreme that I could barely function. I had put my life at risk by not seeking medical advice sooner.

What if I had sought help? Why didn't I? Was it fear, ignorance, or simple avoidance?

After the diagnosis, there was no point in dwelling on the "what ifs." Whatever it was, I had to find a way to put the regrets behind me. I could not imagine putting any energy into feeling guilty or dwelling on the past. Wouldn't that also cause my family and friends to ask themselves why they did not notice my symptoms, and in turn feel a sense of responsibility for my condition? What would be the point in inflicting that on anyone, including myself? I knew that I had to focus on the now.

I invited Susan, my closest friend, out for lunch. In our early twenties, Susan and I had shared a two-bedroom apartment close to downtown Windsor. We had many adventures together, both locally and across the international border, in Detroit. One year living together and countless memories shared between us.

When I broke the news to Susan, we were seated at a table on the patio of a local restaurant. It was a glorious day and I was calmed by the laughter and voices of those seated nearby. I waited until we had finished our meal. Susan was clearly upset when I told her. We have always been honest with each other, and the last thing I wanted was for her to hide her feelings.

I had Yvonne and three other friends to tell in person, and then I could painstakingly make phone calls to others. I wanted them to hear the news directly from me.

Sunday, 21 July

PLEASE keep your narratives to yourselves! It is not in any way helpful to explain what happened to your friend, your brother, your buddy. We are all very different people. Comparing me to someone else only muddles things. I welcome positive energy, laughter, and music in our time together. I can't afford to lose one minute to negativity.

One of my visitors had good intentions, but I was very upset afterwards. She felt it necessary to tell me all about a relative who had been suffering from brain cancer for some time. "He was not supposed to survive this long," she told me, and she even went into detail about his treatments and challenges. I suppose she wanted to give me hope, but at the time I couldn't bear to hear about other sufferers and survivors, especially cancer cases. My "case" was just that — mine. While I had sympathy for her friend, the thought of my tumour being cancerous was terrifying.

Even when we have the best of intentions, it's sometimes all too easy to put our foot in our mouth. When we are not the one living with the diagnosis, it's difficult to know what to say to the person who is. How do we protect and encourage a loved one without causing them additional distress? How do we let them know that they are not alone, and that there is hope? There is no easy answer, and everyone's circumstances are different, but my advice to you is to avoid making comparisons to others' experiences. Instead, focus on your loved one's unique situation, and do your best to make your time together a positive, refreshing, and uplifting experience for them.

———

I had never felt such a total loss of control over my future, my health, or my life. Fear is an intense emotion. The only option was to place my trust in the surgeon and the medical team. However, I did have the ability to control my mindset, responses, personal will, and determination. I believe the intentionality of remaining focused helped me to overcome my fear. Positivity had the power to shield me from the uneasiness or uncertainty of the people who surrounded me.

I had to really work at maintaining this frame of mind while I was faced with physical and mental limitations. I was banned from driving a vehicle, because the risk of a stroke or a seizure was too high. I tried not to think about what could have happened during my 45-minute commute to and from work over the past several months. Someone could have been injured or even killed.

Every one of us can sense when someone is feeling uneasy. We read it through nonverbal signals and actions. We each have our own way of reassuring others, but what's important is that we let them know that we are there for them, and that we will help them find a positive way forward through whatever challenges they may be facing.

Monday, 22 July

Ken has sent an e-mail to his five siblings and his father. They live all across Canada, in Windsor, Kingston, Guelph, Toronto, and British Columbia. We really did not see any other way of sharing this news short of making numerous phone calls. Email was impersonal and I was apprehensive, but we can't bring ourselves to share the information repeatedly on the telephone any more. Selfish.

There was a very real possibility that I would suffer a seizure, but I refused to allow myself to live in fear. To minimize the intracranial pressure, I slept upright on a reclining loveseat in the living room, propped up with pillows.

I scheduled an appointment for a haircut — a ridiculous attempt to maintain some level of control. The result was a refreshing sense of empowerment, however limited it may have been. So much for the concept of texture, colour, style, or appearance!

My relationship with my older children underwent a role-reversal. Shayne became my chauffeur when his father was not available. Marina and I had previously had a typical mother/daughter relationship, which was wonderful at times and combative at others. Now, she moved into the role of a protector, and was frequently checking on me. Mitchell, the youngest, seemed less affected; he continued to play paintball and spend time with his friends and cousin.

The role-reversal seemed inconsequential to Shayne and Marina, but it bothered me. I had always been in full control, almost the task master in our home. I oversaw the schedules, transportation, and communications between us. Watching Shayne and Marina move into these somewhat authoritarian roles was another reminder of my vulnerability. Despite my uneasiness, I needed to let them take charge.

As my sister Colleen prepared to take me to Henry Ford Hospital for a second opinion, she reflected on the experience of learning about my diagnosis.

> Look how much our lives have changed in the last week! I will never forget that fateful phone call. It was a normal busy workday, and I was sitting at my desk, looking out onto the plant floor through the window of my office. The blinds were open as I watched the hustle and bustle during our busy morning operations. When Lynn called, I instantly knew by the tone of her voice that something was very wrong. She tried to assure me everything was alright, but she still wanted to meet to talk. I dreaded what I knew was going to be something bad about my sister, so I insisted that she tell me what was wrong.
>
> The words still ring in my ears. "I have a brain tumour."
>
> What? No! How? Was it cancer? Would it be treatable? I had so many questions but could barely speak. I sat at my desk in sadness and

shock, with tears running down my face, listening to Lynn trying to explain in a methodical and strangely calm way. I really don't remember anything she said, other than the first sentence: "I have a brain tumour."

In an instant, my world had changed. So many things were going through my mind. Lynn was always the one who had taken care of us since we were little. Because Mom was always working, Lynn became a surrogate mother to her three younger siblings. Since Mom died, I have seen Lynn as the matriarch of our family. She was the one I have always gone to when I have needed support, advice, or guidance. Now she is the one who needs her younger siblings to support her through what is sure to be a difficult and most challenging time in her life.

As she tried to console me over the phone, I was crying uncontrollably with my face buried in my hands. I did not realize that the door to my office was open and I was being watched by several employees. One of my supervisors came over and gave me a gentle smile, then closed my door without saying a word.

When I hung up the phone, I sat motionless in my office, just trying to take it all in. A horrible, helpless fear came over me that made me physically sick. I took the rest of the afternoon off. I just grabbed my purse and walked out. I found myself at the cemetery in front of Mom's grave. This is where I go whenever I am feeling sad or overwhelmed with life, and it's where I find peace and strength. I prayed that Mom would watch over Lynn and help her through what was sure to be a very difficult struggle to come.

I think back now at how selfish that was. I should have been consoling her, but as the big sister she had always been, she was more worried about how I would deal with the news. I prayed I had strength for Lynn and for me. I do.

The roles have now reversed. Today, Heather and I are taking her to Henry Ford Hospital in Michigan for a second opinion. It is time to become the big sister for a change, and do what I can do to help Lynn get through the next several months.

My two sisters accompanied me to Michigan for a second opinion. It was such a simple process! I had filled out an online application, and booked my appointment within a day.

We brought copies of all the medical reports, as well as the CD of MRI images for the oncologist's reference. We handed over the information and waited for a short time. He confirmed that the tumour had to be removed without delay, and bluntly stated that it might not be possible to remove it entirely. Pathology results following the surgery, he said, would determine whether the tumour was benign or cancerous. This second, unbiased opinion affirmed the path forward. For a mere fee of $200, we left the hospital with a sense of calm.

Tuesday, 23 July

Mom, I feel heaviness in my heart, as I have daily since the day we lost you 11 years ago. I am reaching out to you and "the gang" to give me strength. Today, I am relieved that you are not here. Is this selfish of me, or a painful glimpse of the horror that a life-threatening diagnosis must inflict on a mother? You had already experienced this once when Heather was diagnosed with Sarcoidosis and a thymus gland tumour in her twenties… the invasive surgery and the aftermath, while her youngest child was still in diapers. I could not look into your eyes again and watch you suffer **with** *worry that would surely be all-encompassing.*

I believed in the power of the mind. During the days before my procedure, I envisioned the tumour being chomped apart, like a Pac-Man devouring his prey. The only alternative would have been wondering, worrying, and focusing on negative possibilities. We spent time with friends who reinforced my positive attitude. Rob and Susan, our long-time best friends, always brought humour and laughter to every get-together. As we floated on rafts around their pool, we joked about giving the tumour a name. "Intruder," "Gate-Crasher," "Freeloader!" they suggested. I enjoyed their spontaneity and humour, but I would not give this "thing" an identity. Never!

Laughter diminishes the worry. When we spend time with friends that have shared so many moments with us, we chuckle at the same jokes over and over again, as outlandish as many are. I felt no burden in the moments when we were reminiscing about when the four of us first met, about our numerous camping expeditions, and our road trips to Florida, along with countless concerts and spontaneous escapades. I had an alliance — a network of strength.

On your own journey to recovery, take time to think about the people who make up your own network of support. Lean on those who bring humour into your life. Laughter really does soothe the soul, and sometimes a good sense of humour can help you see your circumstances in an entirely different light.

Thursday, 25 July

One week from today will be the procedure to tie off the blood supply to the tumour. This could lesson my risks substantially, since the chance of extensive blood loss will be reduced. A week does not seem like a long time, but to me it is an eternity. I am torn. I feel as though I should cherish every moment I have, but I also want this to be done and over with. Time has become both a friend and enemy.

I chose to focus on planning for August 7th, the day of my craniotomy. What would my family do during a full day of waiting? I called Mike, who lives quite close to the hospital. He did not hesitate when I asked if the kids could go back and forth between the waiting area and his home. They could swim, eat some decent food, and pass the time with their cousins, aunts, and uncles. Planning for everyone else allowed me to have control over something.

Saturday, 27 July

I have to prepare myself for the possibilities. If I wake up with no speech function, I will learn again from scratch. If there is a change in my personality, it could be a positive one. If there is a cognitive functioning issue, I'll be in therapy. I can handle any one of these scenarios, and I pray that the entire tumour will be removed. If it is cancerous, my biggest fear will be realized. Radiation or chemotherapy will likely be in my future. I can't dwell on what might be. I'm pulling myself back to focus on today.

A high school friend who lives overseas came by for a visit. Quite frankly, I was not looking forward to it at first, but Annette and I reconnected as we always have, regardless of the time that had lapsed between touching base. She gave me a Reiki treatment to reduce stress and promote healing. I sat comfortably on the couch with my eyes closed as she placed her hands gently on or just above my shoulders, back, head, and torso. She said she was working with universal energy and the energy in my body to promote healing and balance of the seven centres. She tapped into my emotions and into my relationship with my mother. She said I needed to work through a process to let go. Our conversation became one about God and other spiritual teachings. We spoke about countless perspectives from across the world, and agreed that there is something much bigger than ourselves. I felt very refreshed, relaxed, and almost rejuvenated after her visit. Was she meant to be with me that day to help my healing move in the right direction — spiritually as well as physically?

Chapter Three
All Hands On Deck

Sunday, 28 July

I am not afraid of death itself. I believe there is something of an entirely higher nature that awaits me. I don't know what that transformation looks like, but this life is a very small piece of the larger puzzle. I am, however, terrified of the process of dying. Pain? Loss of bodily functions or the ability to communicate? It's the uncertainty of it all.

On the day of my angiogram, I woke with a sense of urgency after a restless night. Will I hear the alarm? What if I'm late? Will it be painful? Will I have to stay overnight? The procedure was going to map the blood flow to and from the site of the tumour, with hopes of cutting off the blood supply. The tumour could then shrink, making the craniotomy the next week much less risky.

My father and siblings were waiting at the hospital when Ken and I arrived. The procedure was explained to all of us, and then two nurses rolled me into a room and placed the bed under a large monitor. The vascular surgeon guided a microscopic camera through my arteries from my groin to the site of the tumour, and he explained what was happening every step of the way.

I felt nothing besides slight sensations. How was that possible when something was being fed through the length of my body, right to my brain? The anaesthesia was just enough to do the trick while allowing me to stay conscious. I was disappointed that I could not see the monitor, so I closed my eyes and tried to picture it.

Heather later shared her experience of waiting for the angiogram to be completed:

Fear had me almost paralyzed. I looked around the room as we waited for Lynn to be called in. Dad, Colleen, Mike, Lynn, and Ken. Lynn, of all people, appeared so in control, with nothing but a "bring it on" attitude. My heart ached. Could they see my fear? Did they feel the same way? What if I never saw my sister again? What if things went wrong that day? Did she know how much I love her? Did she know that I cannot be without her? She is my sister, my strength. Oh my God, I felt so helpless. But the one thing I remember is that I had all the faith in the world in the vascular surgeon. In my eyes, he was an extension to God's hands. If anyone could do this, I knew he could.

So, there we all sat during the procedure, waiting for time to pass. No news was good news. I could feel every beat of my heart. I sensed the fear and anxiety we were all feeling. Me, Dad, Colleen, Mike, and Ken — all connected by the overflowing love we have for Lynn.

Then, there he was! The doctor approached us. He was finished. He had a casual look on his face. "Well," he said, "everything went without incident, but I'm sorry to tell you—" Oh my God, there it was! The news I did not want to hear. I grabbed my heart, afraid to breathe. The doctor said he was not able to embolize the tumour. The main artery that was feeding the tumour was her retinal artery. If he had cut that artery, she would have been instantly blinded. As I looked around, all I saw were people who loved her, all in so much pain and fear — all with eyes tearing up as they tried, like I did to be strong. "Dr. Morassutti is excellent at what he does," he went on to say. "He can handle this."

We waited again... and waited, and waited. Then, the doors finally opened and Lynn was rolled in, awake but still a little groggy. We got to her recovery room, and stood around her bed, numb, with I am sure were long, drawn faces. I can only imagine what she thought. "So, tell me, what did the doctor say?" she asked.

Ken gently explained the outcome of the procedure. Lynn sat up. "So, why all the sad faces?" she exclaimed. We explained. "I'm OK with this," she said. "I certainly did not want to be blind! Now, everyone pull yourselves together, and let's move on with this!"

Amazing. She is unbelievably amazing. Does she know how proud I am to call her my sister?

After a short period, I was taken to a recovery room. The blood that was feeding the tumour was also supplying my left visual field. The surgeon explained that the embolization — the process of cutting off the blood supply to the tumour — had not been done because it could cause total vision loss in my left eye. As Ken briefed me, my family stood beside my bed. My Dad's face turned ashen. He immediately vanished from the room.

My mother's voice spoke to me. "Don't worry or fret over things you have no control over." The chances of extensive blood loss during the surgery were higher, but it was what it was. There was no sense in panicking.

Saturday, 3 August

The positive energy I feel is uplifting and almost inspirational. How is this possible, given that someone is going to remove a portion of my skull in less than a week? Is this denial? Avoidance? I don't care. This is the mindset I choose to embrace.

While I waited for the day of the craniotomy, I did some more research. The Brain Tumour Foundation of Canada (www.braintumour.ca) was an exceptional source of accurate information. As I prepared to undergo my surgery, I learned that there are over 120 different types of brain tumours. 27 Canadians are diagnosed with a brain tumour each day. There are several types of non-malignant tumours, including meningiomas, which is what I thought I had. Meningiomas are tumours that arise from the membranes that surround your brain and spinal cord. The cells multiply out of control to form the tumour. Meningiomas occur most commonly in women in their 40s and 50s, but can also occur in children.

Children. I caught my breath as I continued to read. Perspective makes all the difference in the world.

Possible causes of meningiomas are exposure to radiation, genetic history, or a combination of genetic and environmental factors. I was in the Naval Reserves for 13 years, serving as a Naval Control of Shipping officer. Could the radar on the bridge of our training vessels have been the cause of this tumour? I would never know.

Most people have this kind of tumour at only one site, but it is also possible to have several tumours growing simultaneously in different parts of the brain and spinal cord. Fortunately, I had only one.

I was bold enough to begin watching a demonstration video on the procedure for a craniotomy. The introductory statements were more than enough. "The head is shaved and cleansed with an antiseptic solution. An incision is made and the skin is pulled back. Small holes—" I quickly left the website. What would be the point of knowing every detail of the surgery when I did not have an ounce of control over it?

Sunday, 4 August

Marina's sweet 16th. We had a family party today at our home. The weather was glorious and we enjoyed laughter and conversation out in the yard. Ken relished every moment in front of the BBQ, as he always does. My gardens are now more groomed and beautiful than I could have hoped for. The bright red begonias, multi-coloured impatiens, and hostas are no longer surrounded by weeds. Thank you, everyone!

I now have a much better understanding of the choices my mother made as she fought terminal cancer for three years. She was a proud woman. She never admitted defeat, and refused to speak of the inevitability of her passing. She made that decision for only one purpose: to protect her children. She wanted every day to be a gift.

I respect my mother to this day, but I do wish she had been able to speak more openly about her illness, her feelings, and her hopes. She shut down the conversation whenever any of us broached the subject. I wanted to understand what she feared, and what she believed in, to hold her hand. My mother felt that shielding us from her pain was the right decision. If I am asked a question about my health, my life, my worries, or my convictions I will answer as honestly as I can. In so doing, I am protecting my children, but in an entirely different way. I do not want them to have any regrets about what they could or should have said or done. Life's lessons come to us in many forms.

What would be your approach? Would you discuss your struggles and fears openly? If not, do you think your words might comfort your loved ones, or only cause them to worry or fear for you? What response would you expect from your children, or from your spouse? The answer is different for everyone, and each of us must do what we feel is right at the time.

Chapter Four
Batten Down The Hatches!

Monday, 5 August (morning)

We're sitting in Service Ontario waiting room as Marina finishes her G1 Driver Licence test. She turned 16 yesterday. Wasn't I just learning to drive? It's hard to believe that two of my children are now old enough to get behind a steering wheel. I feel out of sorts, as though I want to hide from public view. It is out of character.

Wasn't it just yesterday that my children were playing in the back yard, covering themselves with sand and water, laughing together? Were we not just bundling them up in their snowsuits to go to Lakeside Park for the Festival of Lights? Had it really been 15 years since we moved 250 km across southern Ontario, from Paris to Kingsville? As I waited for Marina to write her driver's test, I recalled our moving day. Mitchell was less than four months old at the time, and Ken and I were changing jobs. We were relocating to an unfamiliar town with high hopes and expectations. Our mothers and many of our siblings lived in Essex County. We wanted our children to know and love their grandparents, aunts, uncles, and cousins. Our home in Kingsville holds countless memories of us playing, dancing, and laughing together with our extended families.

Monday, 5 August (evening)

I am not so naïve as to believe I am invincible. Should I survive with no cognitive capacity, I am not to be kept alive on a ventilator and fed by tubes. It would be unbearable for our family. I read my legal living will which we wrote the year mom passed away. It left too much room for interpretation. I need to be clear about what I want.

It took me less than ten minutes to put my wishes in writing. As I sat at the kitchen table with the sun cascading through the window, the words came easily. Outside, a cardinal hopped across the lawn beneath the swaying branches of the red maple tree. Cardinals represent energy, vitality, and security as they fly upwards towards the sun. Was this a sign? I smiled as I focused on the page before me.

I was unwavering in my directions to my husband. If Ken had to make the decision to end my life, I wanted him to act in good conscience, with no second thoughts, and with no regrets weighing on him. If ever I cannot breathe or think on my own, I want my family to let me go.

Next, I wrote letters to each of my children. I wanted them to know how proud a mother I am — so proud of what they had already accomplished in their lives, and the difference they would make in the lives of others. Typing with some misgiving, I printed and sealed the letters in envelopes. As I tucked them away, I believed they would be shredded in the not-too-distant future. They would not be needed.

Tuesday, 6 August

I am more than ready for tomorrow. I believe. My surgery will proceed without issue and I will fully recover. I'm tired of waiting. Bring it on, so I can open my eyes and we can put this behind us!

I knew that my family and friends would be by my side the next day. I absorbed their countless positive thoughts, messages, and prayers. They were uplifting. When I closed my eyes and tried to fall asleep, I forced myself to think only about the times when we had laughed until we cried.

Wednesday, 7 August

This is the day I welcome and yet dread. I am being prepped for the craniotomy's nine-hour procedure. Interestingly, I am not afraid. Nor am I dwelling on the details, since I have no control. I feel an unexpected sense of peace, but I am worried for my family and friends, who will be camped out in the waiting area. God, please guide the surgical team today.

The anaesthesia was a blessing. Oblivious to the monitors, needles, intubation, and catheter, I was immobilized for a series of intricate procedures.

My father, Pete, later wrote about a parent's turmoil while waiting during the lengthy craniotomy:

> Pishnook — the roller coaster started when you and Ken told us what was going on. As the conversation progressed, it was evident that our lives were about to change drastically. Your demeanour and straightforward manner as you explained the diagnosis of a brain tumour did not lessen the degree of shock, fear, frustration, and helplessness in my mind. My beautiful, courageous daughter was going through a lot more than what I was hearing about at the time, and you were trying to keep us calm with your assurances that everything was going to be just fine. Bullshit!
>
> For the next few weeks, my mind went through all the possible outcomes, including the loss of my daughter. I could not comprehend — and, to this day, cannot put into words — the fear of losing you, the lynch-pin that made our family so strong. Carol gave me encouragement and reassurance that, no matter what the outcome, we would get through it as a family, and we would draw strength from each other.

When the entire family gathered at the hospital on that frightening day, we were informed that the doctor was hesitant to perform the operation because it was so close to the area of the brain responsible for your eyesight and possibly your hearing. More anxiety and fear of the consequences of doing nothing. The possibility of you going through life not knowing when the fatal day would come, or even if it would, just blew my mind. How could anyone go through something like that and carry on a normal life? Anger was my response. I was angry at God, at the doctor, at myself, and even at you, for letting this happen.

Your decision to go ahead with the operation after your discussion with Ken was one of the most courageous choices any human being could make. I was so proud of you that I thought I would burst — and yet I was fearful of the outcome.

There is no way in hell I could put into words the emotions that went through my brain for the next few hours — fear, anger, total frustration. There was nothing I could do for my daughter, except pray and try to keep the rest of the family thinking positive thoughts. Everything was in the hands of a man I had never met before, and about whom I knew nothing. Is he good at his job? Or, rather, is he exceptionally good at his job? What will my daughter be like when this is all over? Will she change? Will she still function normally? What will my life, her children's lives, and our family's lives be like if something dreadful happens? How can I live with the guilt of letting this happen to you, the one who was always there to help raise the rest of the family?

With the best of intentions, people suggested we should have had the operation performed in the States, because they have better facilities and more advanced technology there. I was angry that something like that was being discussed while you were in surgery. It cast a sense of doubt and fear in the room. You had full faith in your doctor, and without that faith, all the technology in the world would not change the outcome. Your faith in your doctor brought you back to us.

Time passed. After an endless day of waiting and pacing between Mike's home and the waiting room, my cheering section was briefed with the news that the surgery was successful. Family embraced, friends danced, and laughter and tears engulfed the room!

I awoke to see my husband and children standing at the foot of my bed in the intensive care unit. I felt groggy but intensely relieved. I could feel, move, hear, and speak. I even remembered my second language. I wanted to cry, but I didn't. "I can see and hear you," I said, almost giggling. "Je parle français."

Ken was a model of composure. He remained calm and almost light-hearted. The boys, somewhat carefree, told me how they had passed the day. Marina, standing behind her father, was uneasy, but she managed a smile. Susan, Rob, Carol, my father, and each of my siblings visited briefly in pairs. I will never forget these beautiful moments of new-found life.

Marina recalls what it was like to visit me in the ICU for the first time.

> As we sat for hours in the waiting room, many thoughts ran through my head, yet I always came back to one: "Everything happens for a reason." As the doctors announced that the immediate family could see her, I jumped up. They led my dad, brothers, and I past the locked doors of the intensive care unit, and someone started to code. I could hear beeping and other continuous noise, and nurses were running in. I panicked and just wanted my mom.
>
> We walked into her room, and the doctor was there. She looked good for just coming out of surgery, yet at the same time she still looked terrible. It's an image I never wanted to imagine of my mother. I stood behind my dad almost in tears as I began to count the staples in her head. The first words she said were, "I am rocking!" — the sentence we would hear again and again for many months to come.

Chapter Five

Anchors Aweigh

Although I recall only a small portion of what occurred, I know that the intensive care unit was remarkable. The nurses never left my side. I'm told that there were several issues, including my blood glucose levels rising. Hyperglycemia is a dangerous condition that needs immediate treatment to allow the body to perform normal functions. I needed insulin more than once overnight. My blood pressure also dropped as low as 50/48, and it was a challenge to elevate. The nurses responded to each crisis immediately and appropriately.

Once I was stabilized in ICU the next day, I was moved to the eighth-floor neurosurgical unit. One of my nurses assisted me into a wheelchair and rolled me down the hall to a large, accessible washroom for my first shower. I tried to stand and was taken aback at my total lack of physical strength. I had no humility, and was trusting a man I had never met to bathe me, but I couldn't have cared less until I saw my reflection in the washroom mirror. Gauze bandages entirely covered the top and left side of my head. The bruising and swelling were worse than I had anticipated. My head, neck, arms, and various spots on my chest were purple and blue, and had begun to develop a yellow tinge. My face was puffed up so much that my left eye was swollen closed. All of this would heal, I told myself. It is inconsequential.

The next day, my nurse returned to give me a shower. This time, I got out of bed myself with only a little bit of help. He rolled my wheelchair over to the shower and I asked him to leave. He guided me to the stool in the shower stall and gave me the pull cord to call for help if needed. Then, I was on my own. I had everything in a bag beside me, and I took them out and arranged things in the order I would need them — first a cloth, then body soap, then a towel. I wouldn't need shampoo or conditioner. As I showered, I was very cautious to work around the bruising.

After my shower, I decided to get rid of the hospital gown and put on the pyjamas Colleen had given me. I couldn't bend over to guide the pant legs over my feet, so pulled my legs up to where I could reach. Wrapping myself in the towel, I buzzed for the nurse. I admitted that I needed help to pull the top over my head. It was one small step, but a very important one, as I struggled to do what was needed. I was fairly proud of myself as he wheeled me back to my room.

As you navigate through any process of recovery, you must remember how important it is to persist through even the smallest of tasks. If something seems too big to manage, break it down into smaller parts and tackle each part in turn. One little step at a time, you will accomplish much bigger things. As insignificant as these simple strides may seem at the time, they will become great triumphs when you put them all together!

Dr. Morassutti was then doing his hospital rounds. It was the first time I had seen him since the morning of the craniotomy. As he stood beside me, relaxed but purposeful, wearing his white coat, he read my chart and smiled. I looked right into his eyes, reached for his hand, and told him I couldn't find the words to share what was truly in my heart. I did not know how I could possibly say what he meant to me, and to my family and friends. He graciously replied, "That is all I need to hear. Thank you."

As expected, I was very weak, more so on my right side than on my left. My vision was blurred. I wanted to resume doing my journal entries, so I enlarged the font on my computer using the accessibility options, and began slowly typing with one finger. Everything was confusing.

Was my ability to process information impaired? I asked one of my nurses his name countless times, but could not recall his response. I must have had short-term memory loss.

Saturday, 10 August

Each day, more independence, a little bit stronger and farther. I am now able to walk down to the lounge, and have had the pleasure of meeting other patients who have survived similar but also very different experiences. One woman has just undergone her THIRD craniotomy.

The staff on the eighth floor were incredibly kind and caring. I pressed the call button a couple of times one day when I felt my heart beating too quickly. Each time, the nurse came to measure my vital signs and engaged me in calming conversation. He also modelled deep breathing techniques. Then, when I felt the symptoms come back again, I knew what I needed to do on my own.

We can cause ourselves to experience certain physical symptoms when we feel anxious or worried. Our mind will do that to us if we let it, and can even make the anxiety worse. Sometimes, just knowing that we are causing certain symptoms ourselves can help us to overcome them or, at least, minimize the effect they have on us.

Sunday, 11 August

I had no concept of how traumatic the surgery had been until today's cognitive assessment. The therapist asked me to draw a clock. I tried to pick up the pencil, but my fingers felt thick and heavy. The pencil fell to the table, and I tried again. Although I could visualize the image, I could not transfer it to paper. I broke down the process into small steps, but what was supposed to be a picture of a clock looked like a warped hourglass. When prompted to repeat a

series of numbers and words. I was at a loss. How does one
repeat what cannot be recalled? The target score was 26
and I received 23. Disappointing. I am being referred to the
acquired brain injury program for cognition therapy
sessions once my brain has returned to "normal size."
Reminder — this is only four days post-surgery! Again, the
frame of reference matters.

I greatly appreciated the visitors, phone calls, and
messages from aunts, cousins, friends, work colleagues,
and, of course, our extended families. Marina sent me
the most beautiful text on the day of my surgery. She
told me that she was proud of me. Although we had
disagreements from time to time, she acknowledged that
was part of my job as a mom. She knew I was a fighter,
and she said she would be there for me. I cried as I read
those words, and the others that she sent me. In those
moments when mothers and teenagers truly connect, it is
electric. I remained so very proud of my family. And they
needed not worry about their mother any longer — or so I
thought at the time.

Monday, 12 August

I have not seen the area of the craniotomy until today. How
to describe it? Repulsive is the only word that comes to
mind. I have titanium plates holding my skull in place, and
thirty-four staples in my head. Repulsive perhaps, but what
would have been the alternative? A warped smile comes to
my face.

Five days post-surgery, we were given the green light. I
was being released from the hospital. I said farewell to the
uncomfortable bed, and to the interruptions in my sleep.
Colleen had brought a variety of kerchiefs to choose from,
which made me feel much more comfortable. Our friend
Rob waited with us in anticipation as we completed the
final paperwork, reviewed the treatment plan, and

confirmed the future appointment schedule. I would not be going back to work for at least three months, and then my progress would be gauged.

Rob took me down to the main floor in a wheelchair while Ken pulled up the van. The hospital doors slid open and I was swivelled into the sunlight. It was so bright that I winced. Even with the curtains open, a hospital room is drab. Ken chose my favourite radio station for the 45-minute drive home. It was strikingly beautiful in Essex County that day, with a temperature of 28 degrees Celsius. Every moment of the drive, I relished the sight of apple orchards, of perfectly groomed gardens, and of corn, bean, and tomato fields.

As my husband escorted me into our home, I was overcome with emotion and bawled uncontrollably. I was anxious to see, hug, and reconnect with my children. The scent of lavender, the voices I yearned to hear, the beautiful summer colours of yellow and orange blooming in my gardens — never in my life had I ever experienced such intense and overwhelming joy! I had never imagined that walking into our home would bring forth such emotion.

Do you have a memory that plays over and over in your mind? One that you cherish, brings a smile to your face every time? The birth of your children — the moment you first held them in your arms? A conversation with someone you love, who has now passed on? An image from when you were a very young child? As we navigate life's challenges, do not be afraid to replay your fondest memories as often as you need to. Moments and thoughts that give us joy can provide us with an anchor of positive light.

Chapter Six
Mayday, Mayday, Mayday!

Wednesday, 14 August

No bending. No lifting. No walking outside alone. Blurry vision. Everything ringing and humming.

"What's wrong with everyone?" I would often think to myself. Why were they following me around and watching me all the time?

They would say, "Don't do this. Don't do that. Do you need a nap? Don't lift this. Don't bend over." I knew they had good intentions, but it was nauseating. I often wished that they would please just leave me alone to figure this out!

"Leave me alone," I would say one minute. then, the next, "Don't leave me alone!"

My family set up a recovery room in the den near the downstairs washroom, because I could not climb the stairs, but still needed to be carefully monitored. I had a reclining love seat, a side table, and a dresser. Following my body's lead, I slept whenever I felt like it. Most of the time I floated in a fog of fatigue. On the flip side, at times I brimmed with energy and would be awake for hours at night, flicking through the channels on the television. I attributed these rushes to the steroids. My heart raced, and I measured my pulse and blood pressure often. My glucose levels were still elevated, following my reaction on the night of the surgery.

I tormented my family with repetitive expressions. "That rocks!" I often said. "You rock! Let's get rocking!" I didn't know what I was saying from one minute to the next. Thank goodness they were tolerant.

Walking became my solace. I began by walking to the end of the driveway, then part way up the road, and eventually to the end of the street, always escorted by my neighbour, Gabriela, who had become a close friend. Gabriela had countless experiences behind her, having served as a nurse with Doctors Without Borders. She had provided medical aid to people in conflicts, epidemics, and disaster-stricken countries around the world. As we slowly increased the distance we walked to reach yet another goal, we always had something fascinating to discuss. We escaped the reality of each day as we visited Africa, South America and the Middle East in her recollections. Walking with Gabriela was one of the brightest parts of my days.

Sunday, 18 August

Something bizarre and creepy is occurring. The first time it happened, I was perplexed. I can actually feel the healing physically. Over the past three days ... an eerie and repetitive drip, drip, drip in the left upper side of my brain. I smile and cringe at the same time. The swelling is decreasing.

My weight was fluctuating up and down. I was ravenous, even through the night. I soon became obsessed with donating all my clothes because I would never be "that size" again.

Heather and my step-mother, Carol, came to spend the day with me. Before their arrival, I had ignored the doctor's orders and crept up the stairs to our bedroom, and started sorting my closet and drawers. I insisted that they take the clothes for themselves, or donate them as they deemed fit. They cautioned me that I was not thinking clearly, and that I would regret my actions. I didn't care what they thought. I had decided that I didn't want the clothes any longer. That was that. I shoved the clothes into garbage bags. They graciously said they would come back for them in a week's time.

My erratic behaviours and decisions were only just beginning.

Monday, 19 August

What optometrist pays home visits these days? Mine. My vision is horrendous. It doesn't help that I have had 20/200 in one of my eyes since birth. After a full day of work, Dr. McCormick knocked on our door and brought the instruments he needed to measure my eyesight. I need three different prescriptions, depending on what I am doing: one for daily living and watching television, one for working on the computer, and one for reading. We are confident that my vision will improve. He is going to make a pair of glasses with +3.75 dioptre strength, specifically for me. Ken is picking up several over-the-counter pairs at 1.5 and 2.5 that I'll carry in my pocket, since we hope they will only be needed for a very short time.

Vision is one thing. My personality is another. I was now drawn to cooking — something I had, quite frankly, previously avoided whenever possible. It had always been a chore to me, not something I enjoyed. I was now pulling out the recipe books and experimenting. My challenge was having to read and re-read as I prepared the meal, since I could not remember anything from one minute to the next. I began reading aloud, highlighting pages, and continuously double-checking them. One evening, I wanted to barbeque hamburgers. I diligently followed the recipe that Ken had left. I thought I had turned on the barbeque for it to pre-heat, but it was the side burner rather than the grill. I melted the burner lid.

Tuesday, 20 August

I have an overwhelming urge to tell the world of my miracle. I want to scream it from the top of my lungs. Look at me! Look how far ahead of the game I am! At the same time, I am frustrated with my brain capacity, as I seem to be mixed up so often. It is unsettling. In the big picture, this is trivial. If things had gone another way, I would be in therapy now, learning how to speak all over again.

I also felt an urgent need to connect with people. I sent text messages to family and friends in the middle of the night, unaware that my messages were going to their home numbers rather than their cell phones. I'm sure they appreciated the lovely wake-up calls. Shopping on the internet with my credit card in hand was another wonderful way to pass time. I bought a gaming chair, clothes, shoes, jackets, home decorations, and anything else I thought someone needed.

Then, I decided to organize a community event. I thought that I could prepare a presentation that would allow the audience to experience my diagnosis, the weeks leading to the surgery, and this period of recovery. I envisioned my family on the stage with me. In my mind, of course, the residents of Kingsville had nothing better to do with their time but to attend. I wrote the program, booked a date on the calendar, and even began making phone calls to find a venue. I knew it would be a few days before people returned my calls. I waited for responses before going any further.

Wednesday, 21 August

Last year at this time, I was sitting in my beach lawn chair beside Susan, waves splashing on us as they reached the shore. We were spending a week camping at Arrowhead Provincial Park, near Huntsville in the glorious Muskoka region of Ontario. Our teenagers were exploring the park with their friends and cousins who had joined us, fishing, biking, and swimming. We aren't having any of our getaway vacations this year. We've cancelled all three that were planned, and it is such a loss for everyone. Some of our most enjoyable times have been spent around the campfire.

49

exploring trails, rock sliding, swimming, or kayaking.
Breathe. Believe. One road is closed but another will open.

I also worked diligently at re-organizing our home, dumping out the junk drawers, and weeding through stacks of pages that needed to be shredded or filed. I became obsessed with needing everything in its place. Hoping to surprise Ken, I contacted an interior decorator to discuss home renovations, including a workshop and new shed. She and I met several times in prearranged appointments when I thought we could speak confidentially. I spent hours on the phone with a financial advisor attempting to qualify for a line of credit. Ken enlightened me at one point with the total projected cost of my plan. Oh my! So much for the surprise. So much for the project!

Thursday, 22 August

I love dancing! The music is invigorating. I'm dancing in the living room at 4:00 a.m. when Ken arrives home from work. I'm having a blast. I show him an email I had just drafted to friends and family. Join us on vacation in Jamaica in February!

"I'm going to invite Dr. Morassutti, and all the nurses, too." I spiralled around Ken, deliriously happy. "We'll take over the resort!"

Ken closed my laptop. "I'm not sure you'll be well enough to travel by then. Go to bed, Lynn. We'll talk about this in the morning." I now know how brilliant that response was.

Friday, 23 August

I have to tell myself to slow down... to not react. I speak aloud when I put things down, so I don't forget. I have a notebook on the counter to write messages to the family, so I say the same thing to everyone. I need to make it to the next

appointment with Dr. Morassutti on the 17th of September.
I'll have another MRI and know that my brain is healing and
back to its normal size. Three weeks and counting.

The next day, I decided to invite four reporters, with whom I had a professional connection, to a "press conference." I was excited and began cleaning the house and sending text messages to some friends. The world had to know that I was a survivor, and they needed to learn from what I had experienced. My friends immediately reached out to Ken for intervention.

This was the end of my family's patience, and of that of my closest friends. I was sitting on a lawn chair in the front yard when Heather drove up and parked in our driveway. She said that she had cancelled her own patient bookings for the day. She and Ken confronted me with their concerns. I became defensive, and honestly did not understand the situation.

"Do you know that you have spent tons of money shopping on the internet" Heather asked? I didn't care. After they related many examples — bagging my clothes, spending almost $1,000 shopping online in only a few days, planning to redecorate the house, the trip to Jamaica, and calling a press conference — it finally began to sink in.

"Do you want a job to go back to?" my husband stated boldly. They both believed that my body was reacting to the medications and trying to cope with the acquired brain injury.

My sister and husband were gracious as they made telephone calls to extend apologies to multiple individuals. I was upset with them for doing so, and for interfering with my plans. I was still oblivious to the ramifications of my thought process.

They dictated a plan of action for me to type up and sign. I agreed to relinquish all banking and credit cards. Reminder notes were posted around the house: "Do not cook unless someone is with you." "Do not send any emails." "Talk to someone when you think you need something." We agreed that I would refrain from sending any communications, whether by email or text, until they were approved. Phone calls were restricted to only our family members.

Saturday, 24 August

It is burdensome to have no trust in your decisions or instincts. I detest feeling so flustered and tentative. When will this end? I must get beyond the "must have it now" way of thinking. I feel like a bouncing ball — up and down all day and night long. If these mood swings are due to steroids, how do people cope with this for their whole lives? No wonder I cannot think clearly.

I had always taught my children that there is a difference between a "want" and a "need." A materialist approach to life made no sense to me. I had grown up understanding what it was like to barely make ends meet, and had watched my mother make one sacrifice after another. She used to say that she had to "take from Peter to pay Paul" to pay the bills each month. This person that I had become was not me.

The boat was taking on water. I couldn't read. It was a frightening revelation in the midst of a day planned for relaxation at the home of Helen, a friend of almost 15 years. Lounging on lawn chairs beside her pool, entertained by branches of the trees swaying to and fro, I enjoyed the sounds of cardinals singing their two-part whistles. As I turned the pages of my James Patterson novel, it became abundantly clear. I had no recollection of what I had just read, not even after I read it aloud the second time. One of my treasured life pleasures had been stolen from me. I suppose I should have been happy that I still had the ability to decipher individual words and phrases. But at the time, I wondered what the point was when the words still didn't connect to form meaning? Helen, always the voice of positivity, suggested we enjoy a game of Scrabble. We were seated at the patio table with the sun shining upon us. It was a brilliant attempt to redirect my attention, until we realized that I could only create two- and three-letter words. My frustration quickly ended the game.

We couldn't stem the leak in the boat. During a basic conversation regarding automobile insurance for my oldest son, Helen and her husband were giving me advice. A moment later, I had no recollection of what we discussed, even after she repeated herself. I sensed that I was asking the same questions over again. I decided to write down both the questions and the answers. At least it could be read by someone if I couldn't remember. I could have screamed.

Life jacket, please!

Tuesday, 27 August

I can't drive. I can't read. I can't remember anything from one moment to the next. I can't see or hear clearly. I can't deal with this!

Stop.

I can walk. I can speak. I can laugh and smile. I can feel. I must stay positive. I need to focus on what I can do as opposed to what I can't. I must figure out a way to deal with my limitations. Everyone does. I am no different.

What seemed like such a small setback to anyone else could have been the final straw for me.

During times when we are still celebrating being able to sit up in bed, then to take five steps across a room, and then down a hallway, the goal of independence can seem so distant. Tiny steps forward are just that — they are tiny. Just don't let yourself or someone you are caring for lose hope. Thinking about where you want yourself or a loved one to be in six months' time will serve no purpose except to frustrate you. Sometimes, you just have to accept that it's just too far away from your grasp. Focus instead on what you can do for them and yourself today.

That Thursday night, I felt cold to the core under a fleece blanket. My arms and neck became inflamed, red, and itchy. A rash began to spread across my body, and then I felt too hot and threw the blanket aside. I had mixed feelings about the state I was in, but did not wake anyone up. Instead, I wrote everything down to share in the morning.

I wondered what was happening. I had begun taking Tylenol every four hours the day before, due to an ongoing headache. My left temple was throbbing and the pain spread across my forehead. When I told my husband in the morning, he reminded me that this was one of the symptoms they had warned us about — a possible brain bleed. He was visibly upset that I had not woken him.

En route to the hospital by ambulance, my blood pressure skyrocketed and fluctuated. The attendant skilfully used humour to distract me. I welcomed the morphine in the emergency department as I waited through the night for a CT scan and chest X-ray.

Friday, 30 August

What a night! I have such respect for the medical profession after what I have witnessed over the last several hours. I was in the corner of the ward with a view of the cubicles ahead of me. A man strapped into a bed not far from me shouted obscenities until the police escorted him away. A woman who clearly had dementia walked towards a nurse and actually struck him in the chest, barking accusations as she did so. At the same time, a teenager repeatedly screamed sexual comments towards another nurse, and even invited him into bed with her! How awful for someone to be in such an intoxicated state, and unpleasant for those who have no choice but to respond. The staff were nothing but calm and purposeful in each situation. These people deserve recognition for what they endure as part of their jobs.

Dr. Morassutti has a clinic in the hospital. I was released from the emergency department and directed there. My neurosurgeon and nurse were sitting across from us on the other side of a table in the meeting room. They had spent a great deal of time analysing the information before them. The CT scan that was done overnight revealed that most of the edema had dissipated, as had been expected. They had determined that the prescription of Keppra, which I was taking for seizures, had caused a reaction they had not witnessed before. The rash was a result of my body's withdrawal from Decadron, the steroid. I had been decreasing the dosage, but clearly it needed to be decreased much more slowly, and over a longer period of time. These symptoms, combined with my bizarre, out-of-character behaviour over the past while, resulted in a diagnosis of "extreme mania."

"You can expect the erratic behaviours to continue for up to three more weeks," the doctor said as he handed me a new prescription. He stood up from his swivel stool and acknowledged our safety plan, reiterating how lucky I was to have such strong support.

My first reaction was to feel sorry for myself. "Why me?" I thought. "Why all these first-time road blocks?" I felt as though my boat was continually being rocked by new and totally unexpected waves.

I thought of my mother and her three-year battle. I reassured myself that the mania was only expected to last for a few weeks. When I think back to those long days when my family could not predict my words or actions, I realize how stressful it must have been for them. I became someone else. The hardest part followed: knowing and dealing with it, losing and regaining control, and checking with others who were still logical to ensure I was on the right track.

Getting past the "gotta have it now!" impulse was not easy, since I lived a continuous cycle of hyperactivity and grandiose notions countered with disorganization, irritability, and poor judgement. I cannot imagine permanently living with that mindset. I typed a message to a friend on Facebook Messenger, which I felt was secure and private. As I hit the "Enter" key, I felt guilty. I had broken my contract. At that time, it was almost impossible to force myself to stop. It was like an addiction.

When you are caring for another person, remember that the person you are supporting is facing their own personal weaknesses, along with the medical conditions from which they are recovering. For many patients who are independent and strong-willed: look out!

When we are patients ourselves, accepting and welcoming support can actually make us feel as though we are being forced to accept defeat. There comes a point in time where we come to understand that pushing people away will only serve to delay our healing. It is frustrating, and it can be a struggle. Whether we are the caregivers or the ones being cared for, we all need patience to steer through this turmoil.

As Marina explains, she found it particularly difficult to adjust to the "new" me.

> My mom was home. She was not normal. Her behaviour was chaotic, scatter-brained. Her cognition and attention span was like that of a child. Since I was in charge while my dad and older brother were at work, she often yelled at me and became easily temperamental — and understandably so, since I'm her child, not her mother. She did not enjoy listening to my rules, but also often apologized for getting upset. I could tell she was annoyed because she could not do most things alone, and she often needed help. I tried to be as caring and compassionate as possible, while still giving her space. She was not allowed to text or use social media without permission.
>
> One morning, I went outside to check on her. She was sitting on the patio, using the phone. I immediately had to tell her to hang up. She had answered a call without permission. She was furious that her 16-year-old daughter was telling her what to do. I took her phone away. I felt guilty, but knew it was the right thing to do. Then I knew what it must be like to raise a child. They may be furious with you at times, but in the end, you are protecting them.

As weeks went by, with the help of friends and family, she began to get better. She wished she could cook dinner on her own and was mad when I tried to help. The dinner turned out horrible, but out of respect I pretended to love it. The smile she had as I choked down the food and pretended to like it was all worth it. It gave her that sense of hope and independence she yearned for.

When someone is behaving irrationally, or being stubborn or difficult, they are in their own emotional "place." Their behaviour is a result of their personal background and experiences. They might be dealing with something of which we have no knowledge at all. If you are caring for someone like that, just take some time to listen to them, with patience and empathy. Try to take a walk in their shoes. They will usually be glad to know that someone is at least trying to see things from their point of view.

Saturday, 31 August

I enjoyed two walks today and I am getting much stronger. I've fallen into a routine of napping mid-day for as long as I need to. I am able to cook if I am watched. Phone calls are allowed, and I have been more active on social media, although mostly lurking. None of this occurs without caution and nervousness. I am still so unsure of myself, but pleased that some of my restrictions have been lifted. The kids have been watchful — a little too bossy sometimes, but I am rolling with it.

Many years ago, I visited a teacher to deliver some cards and gifts after she had been diagnosed with breast cancer. When she heard the news of my diagnosis, she left a card in our mailbox with a lovely note and a charm. It wasn't until I read the note that I remembered that it was the same charm I had given her ten years before, at a time when she was fighting her own illness. It was a real-life example of "What goes around, comes around." What might seem to you like a small gesture or gift can be profoundly meaningful to someone who is dealing with one of the greatest struggles of their lives.

Sunday, 1 September

The family threw me a party today at my sister Colleen's home. The weather could not have been more glorious. My siblings and their families from Essex County and Michigan, aunts, uncles, my father, stepmother, and our dearest friends all joined us. There had to be at least 50 people, and my cousin's band played for us. Dad had arranged for his annual fish fry with perch from a friend in Wheatley. Many enjoyed a day of swimming, horseshoes, water fights, and great conversation. What a blast! The volume of the music soared in my ears. I knew I would have to sneak out to the front yard at times. To my surprise, it also gave me ample opportunities to connect with people individually. I even helped my niece write her resume!

My father, a gifted musician, joined the band to sing a few songs. As he moved around with the microphone in his hand, we sang along to "Sweet Caroline." I enjoyed every moment and remembered most of the words.

The neighbours behind Colleen's home gathered in their own yard to enjoy the music. I thought I would go over and say hello, even though we had never met. As I danced across the lawn towards them, Rob asked me what I was doing. He said I needed to come back to the party. Feeling like a child being scolded by a parent, I told him, "I am angry with you right now." I guess I did sound like a child, so why not treat me as one? It seemed that wherever I went, someone was checking up on me and asking if I was okay. I wanted them to have fun, not feel as though they had to be my guardians. I knew that everyone meant well. I was still confused, but was also determined to heal. When we move forward faster than we should be, we may get upset when people are trying to slow us down. Just know that you might be in for an earful!

Chapter Seven
Harness The Wind

In September, Shayne, our eldest son, returned to Guelph to begin his second year in genetics and microbiology. Even as a pre-schooler he was remarkably inquisitive. "Why does it rain?" he would ask. "How does the moon move?" He had such a scientific mind! He was always destined to be a researcher, I had no doubt about it.

I missed him already. On the first day of school, as I waved good-bye to Mitch and Marina, I felt lost, but also delighted at the same time. Other than during my maternity leaves, I had never been home in the mornings to enjoy these moments. I was excited for them, and hoped the school day would bring them everything they hoped for.

Tuesday, 17 September

Happy 15th Birthday Mitchell, and a gift at today's appointment. I had jitters leading up to today's consultation, and for no reason. The tumour wasn't cancerous! The pathology confirmed it as a benign meningioma. This was the news I had been waiting for. The sense of relief takes my breath away.

My brilliant neurosurgeon sat down on a stool across from the hospital bed where I had been waiting. He said that the entire tumour had been removed, and that no chemotherapy or radiation was necessary. I was sure I would have been referred to an oncologist much sooner if it had been cancerous. He explained that he had needed to cauterize the spot where the tumour had touched my optical nerve, which meant that he had used a heated instrument to burn the area so there would be no further bleeding or infection. My MRI that morning showed that my brain was back in alignment, with very little edema. It was an excellent recovery. However, I would continue to need MRIs done on a regular basis as a proactive measure, since this type of tumour still has a 17 percent chance of recurring.

I wanted to scream with joy at the top of my lungs. I had won another round!

My life would now involve routine MRIs, more often during the first three years of recovery. It was the first time we saw the images of the titanium plates that were holding my skull intact. They resembled small staples forming a circle around the surgical site. Fascinating.

Wednesday, 18 September

I read a copy of the clinical notes that had been prepared following our first appointment with the neurosurgeon. "She understands that by not removing the lesion it will continue to grow. The increasing edema will eventually cause her to lapse into a coma and die."

I paused and read on.

"She understands the risks and benefits of the surgery include but are not limited to the possibility of death, myocardial infarction, pneumonia, possible DVT and pulmonary embolus, infection, haemorrhage, possibility of paralysis and stroke and the possible recurrence of the tumour."

The decision to have the surgery was made so quickly, but it was the rational one. There clearly was no alternative.

The next day, only six weeks post-surgery, I walked 5 km in the McGregor Mug Run. My nephew Ryan is the organizer for this annual community fundraiser, which begins with the run and is followed by a craft beer festival. Many members of the family volunteered. Heather was on call to respond to anyone with medical needs. Colleen and I waited at the starting line, positioning ourselves behind the real competitors. As Ryan counted down with the megaphone, it was exhilarating. We were off! Within moments of starting, we fell behind most of the other participants, but could not have cared less. We passed each of the volunteers who marked the path along the route, first through the town and then following the Chrysler Greenway. Our speed "walk" was completed in 45 minutes or so. As we grew closer to the inflated archway that marked the finish line, we could see and hear many people cheering. I picked up the pace and crossed the finish line with Colleen beside me. I threw my hands in the air, teary-eyed and proud. My heart pounded in my chest as I shook. It was such an emotional moment, crossing the finish line surrounded by cheers from many who waited for us. Such an empowering experience!

Saturday, 21 September

For over 25 years now, Ken has enjoyed an annual fishing trip with several other OPP officers. He leaves tomorrow for five days. He did not make the decision to go until just today, because of his concern for me. We turned a corner today, a pivotal moment in time. I am so relieved. Gabriela will be coming to walk with me daily, and the kids are home from school by 2:45. We have arranged for a daily visitor and I know what my plan is. It's also written down so I can't forget.

―――――――

Ken and I met for an assessment with Dr. Strang, a neuropsychologist. He put into clinical terms what I had been living with since the surgery: poor memory registration and short-term recall, mild object-naming weakness, lack of self-monitoring and inhibitory control, and impaired executive function in decision-making. None of these diagnoses surprised us. He explained how my brain worked, and specifically how mine had been traumatized. He recommended that I:

+ be patient during recovery, as my brain needed time to form new connections;
+ gradually replace daytime naps with planned rest periods and downtime;
+ intersperse challenging activities with routine activities;
+ take care of my emotional health by including "fun times" in my weekly schedule;
+ maintain a balance of physical and cognitive activities that are mildly challenging and would build endurance;
+ learn to use technology to assist with memory and scheduling;
+ clarify information at the time it is received, to ensure understanding and to provide an opportunity for mental rehearsal; and
+ continue to work on strategies to categorize new information.

What a relief to understand why things were happening, and to have charted a clear course forward!

Monday, 7 October

How refreshing it was to visit the salon and leave with my hair an even colour and length. There was so much grey in the little hair I had. I have no idea where that came from. I look forward to shelving my collection of headbands and bandanas, which will be a symbolic occasion and another step forward. The "chipmunk" cheeks I have developed are an entertaining change. I expect that my facial features will return to normal when the effects of the steroids wear off.

I experienced a welcome turn of events while at Windsor Regional Hospital with Heather. I was spending time in the cafeteria while she attended a meeting, and decided to make a proactive phone call. I had been scheduled for an EEG in six weeks' time to measure for seizure activity. I called the department to ask if my name could be placed on a waiting list for the first available opening. I was in the right place at the right time, and was invited to go up immediately. The nurse was very pleasant, and explained that I was going to lie down on the bed and be exposed to various colours and patterns of lights that would flash before me. She placed sensors in the appropriate locations to measure my response. How intriguing! I was not nervous or uncomfortable. The results would be shared at my next appointment.

By this point in the recovery process, the scars on the side of my face had turned crimson and blue, and the itching was intolerable. Oatmeal baths, calamine lotion, Benadryl, and anti-itch cream all had no effect. I had had an MRI earlier in the day. Could I have been allergic to the dye used during the MRI? Once again, I found myself in the emergency department that evening, this time in Leamington. The physician could not confirm what caused the allergic reaction, but prescribed a steroid to combat the effects. More steroids — the last thing I wanted.

Thursday, 24 October

The little hair I have is falling out. I was very upset at first, but I remembered Mom. She asked us to shave her head following her diagnosis of lung cancer. Mom did not know her future and was beginning chemotherapy. She put her hair in a tree so the birds could use it to make their nests.

Refer to me as the Head Band Queen — again.

A "poor me" attitude serves no purpose except to delay, halt, or impede recovery. I am a true believer in the mind–body connection. In those moments when I felt defeated, I reminded myself that negativity can serve no real purpose in recovery. No one wants to be around a miserable person who is self-destructive. That person, in the end, is only doing harm to themselves and those around them.

If you don't believe you can reach the goals you set for yourself, you won't reach them. If you believe you can, and you take small steps, you will get there eventually. Don't dwell on the end of the road — it's too far away, and it will seem as though there are too many hurdles in your path. Focus on one day or one smaller challenge at a time. Sometime in the future, you will be able to look back and celebrate how far you have come.

If you ever have a friend, colleague, or relative who is facing a life challenge, do not flinch. As awkward as you may feel around them at times, and as uncertain you might be about what to say, just be there for them. It makes all the difference in the world. Accept that they will never be the same. Even after a full physical recovery, the challenges they are facing are also powerfully influential both emotionally and spiritually.

If your loved one is experiencing an acquired brain injury, welcome the new person and the new personality that you meet. Throw up a fresh set of sails for them. Let them know that they do not have to face this challenge alone.

Chapter Eight
Ready About

Sunday, 27 October

It's time to venture into the gymnasium and arena. Marina has a basketball game at the school tomorrow, and Mitch plays hockey this weekend. I'm not sure I can handle the whistles or roar of the fans in the stands, but I have missed cheering them on so much this year. I love going to their games. They haven't said anything, but I think they miss me being there.

I was very nervous as I walked to the school. I forced myself to take some deep breaths. Marina had stayed after school for warm-ups before the game, and I was walking alone. I entered the school and was greeted by parents from the team, who were running the canteen. Inside the gym, music blared. Marina was taking a shot and she smiled as she ran past me. Perfect timing. I needed that!

I scanned the stands to find fellow parents I would be comfortable sitting with, and steered the conversation toward events in their lives. What a relief when the whistle blew and the game began. At the end of the second quarter, the noise level was almost unbearable, and I needed to step out. I did not want to disappoint Marina, so I eventually returned to the gym, but I stood near the door for the remainder of the game. The hockey game was in a few days, and I cheered Mitch on from the viewing area in the arena lobby, as opposed to sitting in the stands. I positioned myself in the lobby intentionally so that I was away from other people, and shielded from the noise. I had totally forgotten that the boys rang the puck up against the acrylic glass in warmups. Nothing to do but laugh after I jumped out of my boots.

Monday, 4 November

Hallelujah! I am being weaned off the Keppra! My neurosurgeon does not want to see me for six months because I am doing so well. The recent EEG and MRI results were excellent. I asked if I could sleep in my own bed, with my husband. He smiled and said I only needed to keep my head slightly elevated. When I asked him about the hair loss, he replied, "It doesn't happen to many of my patients, but you are a lucky one." He is genuine, that is certain.

It was important for me to acknowledge and thank the many medical professionals involved in my diagnosis and treatment. I painstakingly wrote formal letters to the Windsor Regional Hospital managers, the Minister of Health, the Chief Officer of Health, three MPPs, one MP, and the president of the College of Physicians. I also wrote a letter to each of the nurses, Dr. Morassutti and my optometrist who had visited my home to assess my vision loss. I wanted to recognize them. The act of writing "thank yous" can even help us put into perspective just how large a support network we really have.

Some of my former colleagues had been making contact. Speaking and meeting with them was an important step forward. I was beginning to think rationally, and I focused on working out at the gym and walking so I could become physically stronger. The rest would fall into place in time.

My confidence was growing and I wanted to start driving again. But how would I react in unforeseen circumstances — for example, if an animal ran out in front of my car? I sought permission from the neuropsychologist and my family physician. Both fully supported me getting behind the wheel, but only for short distances within town. After three months of being dependent on others, I now had freedom at my fingertips!

Friday, 15 November

Trepidation. I adjust my rear-view mirror, both frightened and exhilarated. Backing out of the driveway with the intention of going to Lakeside Park, I start to laugh. I don't stop at the park but drive around town with the sun roof open, the wind ruffling my bandanna. I am carefree — alone!

We had been looking forward to a road trip back to the Brantford area. Ken and I lived there for 10 years, and still have many close friends there. They're the sort of friends where months can pass without talking, but when you pick up the phone, it's like you had just spoken yesterday.

We first met Lorri, Kevin, Sandy and Rob in our mid-twenties, just beginning our careers. Then came the marriages and children. We had a reunion planned for the next weekend, and I had collected several photos of times spent with our babies and toddlers at each of our homes. Ken and I had always hosted an annual party on Canada Day. The Paris parade went right past the front of our home, and the fireworks were held at the fairgrounds behind our property. It seemed like yesterday. Lorri had a bottle of wine put aside for us. It was a very special toast to health and our futures, and my first sip of alcohol in almost four months. We then stopped in Guelph on the way home to visit Shayne and his two new roommates

Four months after the craniotomy, however, I felt as though I was on a decline. I searched online about what to expect at this stage, but the information on the medical websites seemed to cover only the first three months. I had a constant feeling of weight on the left side of my head, inside and out, which worsened as I grew tired. Was the leaden feeling linked to scar tissue or the titanium plates? My vision also seemed to be deteriorating. Was a tumour growing again? As I contacted my neurosurgeon's office for a consultation, I remembered the woman I had met who had endured three craniotomies. The nurse who worked with me regularly was sympathetic, and reminded me that my recent MRI scan showed that everything was healing as it should be. My body had gone through an extensive trauma and these symptoms were to be expected. She also reiterated that it was only four months post craniotomy — a very short time. I was O.K.

Tuesday, 3 December

Long Term Disability... not something I ever wanted to consider. I received a letter today stating that my application was due by the beginning of January. What a kick in the teeth. I had planned on being back at work by now. I can't imagine that someone recovering from the removal of a brain tumour would be denied. It's all about companies making money, though. If LTD were denied or even delayed, I will have no income. That's not something I even want to think about. We've got to get the application done right away.

I reached out to Dr. Strang in hopes of scheduling an assessment at the beginning of January, so I could return to work, even part time. He said he was not comfortable doing the assessment until at least six months following the surgery, which took us to February. I was upset. I hung up the phone and vented to Ken. He has always been calm and rational, and he fully agreed with Dr. Strang. If I went back to work too soon and made poor decisions, I would quickly lose credibility. I could not take that risk.

Wednesday, 11 December

I may not be able to work, but I can most certainly have a social life. I enjoyed a wonderful breakfast at Cora's this morning with colleagues who are leading the department in my absence. They are hopping, with never a dull moment.

Memories and a flash of reality. After an hour with them, I know that I am absolutely not ready to return. The pace alone would be too overwhelming. Two more months might make all the difference in the world.

Was I to just sit back and take the ride, or make every day the best that it could be? Some people believe there is a pre-determined destiny for each of us. This may very well be, but I believe we can also alter our destiny through the choices we make, whether good or bad. Choosing to change our path means that we can take action to do so. Sitting back and watching the world go by is a waste. It will leave you high and dry.

Wednesday, 25 December

It is 10 o'clock on Christmas Day, and we are patiently waiting for our teenaged children to rise. Things certainly have changed as they have gotten older. No more milk and cookies for Santa, listening for the patter on the roof at night, or 6 o'clock wake-ups. I do miss those times, but these are also new and exciting. I can now look forward to future Christmas celebrations with my grandchildren — someday.

I cherish the moments of hanging the decorations that our kids made while they were growing up — bulbs, popsicle sticks, stickers, and such. I have such vivid memories of my childhood at this time of year, too. The gifts were not what was important. It was the family gatherings, singing with my cousins as my aunt played the piano on Christmas Eve, listening to the radio to hear where Santa was, and sharing a wonderful brunch in the morning. My most vivid memory is of the year when we were living with our five cousins, after having to move out of our home when the interest rates skyrocketed. Nine of us shared beds in my aunt and uncle's Wheatley home. Can you imagine nine children sneaking around before dawn? Presents filled the entire room, right up to the door. There was chocolate milk to go around, and laughter and excitement from children between the ages of three and ten. It seemed that it didn't matter, either to us or to our parents, how crowded the place was. Such a pleasant memory!

Four months after my craniotomy, we enjoyed two amazing Christmas celebrations, one for each side of the family. With Ken's five siblings, we had about twenty-five people. The Prior clan has just as many. We laughed together both nights. The best part has always been when the cousins come together and reconnect. We were living mom's legacy. She was our guiding light. "There is nothing as important as family." She said and lived this sentiment regularly.

The values we all learn as we grow up can help each and every one of us through the ups and downs in life. In the most trying of times, we should hold true to those teachings.

In the lull between Christmas and New Year's, I organized the binder where I kept all my medical records. I had a flashback to where it all began, and a confirmation of just how far I had come.

Sunday, 29 December

I had obtained a copy of my "Operative Report" from Patient Records. The craniotomy was outlined, step by step. "The patient was brought into the Operating Room in an urgent scheduled manner and the preoperative checklist was reviewed and verified by the OR team before proceeding ... The patient was then placed in the supine position ... in a three-point Mayfield head fixation. Using the Z-touch system, the Brain Lab navigation system was registered to the patient's facial features ... The muscle and scalp were then reflected inferiorly and anteriorly ... A bur hole was then made..." If I had studied these details prior to my surgery, I would have been terrified. Today, with intrigue, I read the report thoroughly, checking the medical jargon with an online dictionary.

We hosted a New Year's Eve Party with an open invitation to our neighbours and friends. It was the least we could do to thank them for their support. Saying farewell to 2013 was cause for one heck of a celebration! There was so much food that we wouldn't need to cook again for several days, and we were entertaining company until 3 o'clock in the morning. As I moved throughout the main living/dining area, offering beverages and joining in conversations, I paused to take it all in. Every person in our home had their own story, their own heartaches, and their own celebrations. Was one more or less significant than the other? Based on our own experiences, perceptions, hardships and tragedies, each of us might answer this question differently. What is important to remember is that people are what make the world go around. If we did not have each other, what really would matter?

Wednesday, 15 January

Things are returning to my new normal. Yes, I do have a temper that flares up occasionally, as my youngest does not hesitate to point out. From my point of view, people know how to press those "buttons." Of course, I know nothing and they are the wizards. It's best to walk away, rather than engage in an argument which will only exacerbate the situation. The fact that I am able to do so says a lot.

What is it all about, anyway? Everyone wonders this from time to time. If everything happens for a reason, how do we explain the passing of a child? How do we rationalize the fact that children get cancer? Why do bad things happen to good people? Is there something greater than us? Do spiritual beings exist in human form?

I once listened to a speaker who shared his belief that we live multiple lives to reach our full potential, and that before we re-enter this physical life, we make decisions about the lessons our spiritual beings still need to learn. The lessons could be of compassion, grief, fear, humility — there are countless possibilities. We might even be here for just a short time, he said, for the sole purpose of teaching others.

His view of life might be one way to help others cope with tragic loss. If a spiritual being chose to enter the world briefly, as an agent of learning or grace, then there really would be a purpose to a life cut short. But what if, once in physical form, the spiritual being deviates from the chosen path?

These conjectures are far removed from how I was raised as a Catholic. It is fascinating to explore the different beliefs and cultures from all around our world — yet each time I learn something new, more questions come forward.

Thursday, 13 February

What a day! I am very fatigued after six hours of cognitive testing. It has been months since the neuropsychologist first gave me recommendations. This time, I felt pressure to prove that I was well enough to return to work. I wanted him to see that the action items he gave me have worked. In a small room, he and a psychometrist took turns giving me the tests.

Believe it — six hours with only 45 minutes for a lunch break!

"So, I understand you want to go back to work," said the neuropsychologist. We were meeting in his office. He referred to his notepad. "Do you have any concerns?"

I was worried about short-term memory, fatigue, stress, making a fool of myself, and returning too soon.

"My short-term memory isn't very good," I answered, and I explained the strategies I had put in place, such as taking notes.

He supported my decision to return to work three days per week. But if I felt tired or stressed, or if the headaches returned, I should pay attention. Those would be signs that I was doing too much, too fast. I was to send him a report each week so that he could monitor my progress. He said he would give me feedback on my short-term memory test, complete with scoring, the next week.

I felt a sense of relief, but I was also cautious and certainly not as confident in myself as I had been in the past. Does our ego lead us to believe that we are irreplaceable at work? Clearly, this notion is far removed from reality. Regardless of the reason for an absence, someone else steps in and the job carries on.

I was anxious to return to work, but with an entirely new mindset. I questioned whether my career drive and aspirations had stolen my ability to keep my family and friends in the forefront.

When our children were young and Marina was diagnosed with asthma, we decided to hire someone to come into our home when both of us were working during the day. Ken's continental shift allowed him to often be home during the week. Tammy, who became a dear friend, gave our children the love and care they deserved when we were not able to be at home. But should that have been me, instead?

The neuropsychologist informed me that my assessment showed "significant improvements." Corresponding test results yielded an "average to above-average" cognitive level. With these standardized assessments, I now had evidence of the remarkable improvement that I had made both cognitively and emotionally. This time, he made only two recommendations, each related to my return to work:

- ✦ Lynn is ready to return to work to her very challenging job on a graduated basis. I recommend three (3) days per week to start: Monday, Wednesday and Friday. This will allow for information and experience consolidation, strategy implementation, recovery, and the opportunity for self-evaluation of her functioning on the off-work days and at the end of the week.
- ✦ It is further recommended that Lynn's return to full time work be determined based on evaluation of findings from her weekly reports, which I will monitor and review with her.

I understood how important that affirmation was, given the past seven months of goal-setting, setbacks, and tiny steps forward. I also fully understood that if I did not follow these recommendations, I risked taking a step back in my recovery. I could not make decisions unilaterally, and would be working side-by-side with a remarkable woman who had agreed to step into my position with no warning or proper transition.

Chapter Nine
Plotting The Course

Friday, 14 February

Mitch and I were in the car driving to hockey practice last night, talking about everything happening for a reason. I asked him what he thought the reason was for my tumour. He hesitated, but then said maybe I needed time off work to get rid of the stress. I suggested that it has given us time to come together as a family. He laughed and said I am short-tempered now, and I jump all over him about little things. Is he right? I sure hope not. I would agree that I have always had high expectations for my children. They are too intelligent and have far too much potential to expect anything less. Mitch has given me reason to reflect. I will be much more aware of my temperament.

I was beyond nervous about the "return to work" meeting with my supervisor, the human resources, and the disability officers. How would I stroll back into my job after being away for so long? I had no idea what had happened in anyone else's lives. My focus had to be on my role, and on reconnecting with so many people. I had planned to ask a colleague to explain that I preferred not to discuss the last seven months of my life. I wanted to get on with things.

Thursday, 20 February

Another milestone reached! I had my "back to work" meeting today. I am very blessed to have such a wonderful group of people to work with and to work for. After the meeting, I made a point of visiting people. I hoped it would lessen my anxiety before "officially" starting on Monday. I was visibly nervous, and even shaking at first. After a few hugs and welcomes, it became much easier.

My first official day at work threw me right back into the thick of it. It seemed as though five issues came at me one after another. I was able to keep focused on one thing at a time, putting items aside that were not a priority. I could see how everyone felt under pressure, and wanted immediate responses to things that were in no way critical. There were so many things I did not know, but I made no decisions without consulting with our supervisors or administrative staff. I was thankful for the sense of humour that was still very much present in my workplace.

Monday, 24 February

It struck me in the middle of the morning: I have no recollection of the legislation, policies, or procedures I am bound by. I had suspected that my memory would be a hindrance to my work, but this is an enormous hurdle. On my days "off," I will be rereading and tabbing everything I need for reference at my fingertips. I now also must learn how to use the Office 365 Suite. Lord help me!

On my days off, when I felt as though I was being pulled down, I would scan through the photos of the week after my craniotomy. They are clear and vivid reminders of where I was, and of an experience that I hope to never have to go through again. I would also pull out the box of cards and letters that so many people had sent. In the months of my recovery, I had read them over and over, always as if for the first time.

Most people now prefer to communicate electronically — whether by email, Facebook, or through the latest trendy social media sites and apps — instead of sending a hand-written note. Trust me, mailing or delivering a card or gift to someone with a brain injury brings them joy repeatedly!

Wednesday, 19 March

A reminder: I am still recovering. I lost control and bawled my eyes out in front of approximately 80 people today. I was overwhelmed with emotion.

When I arrived at a large-scale monthly meeting, the room was arranged as it always had been, in circular tables of eight. People were speaking with each other, moving around, getting a coffee to start their day, and arranging their materials. I nervously shifted from table to table with greetings, extending smiles, and hugs. I had not seen many of them since last June, when I had wished them an enjoyable summer. My new supervisor welcomed me publicly and then made beautiful comments about my journey. Everyone rose from their seats to give me a standing ovation. I put my head in my hands and cried. I was overcome by a staggering sense of relief, pride, and even triumph.

At first, I was annoyed with myself for revealing my vulnerability to the people I work with and lead. But we are all human, and we need to be reminded of that occasionally. Perhaps my response helped others realize that they, too, must count their blessings, and that each of our lives can change in the blink of an eye. I was past being embarrassed. It was what it was.

Eight months post-surgery, I had an appointment with my neurosurgeon. It was interesting how quickly things seem to fade into the background and then WHAM! — you are kicked in the teeth and reminded of the misery you've been through.

Ride the wave. It will subside.

He broke it to me that it would be a full two years before my brain would be totally healed and I understand the "new me." He said he believed the tumour took years to grow into the size it was, first slowly but then aggressively. The short- and long-term memory issues I was experiencing were to be expected. The weight I felt behind my left eye was also part of the healing process. He reminded me that my brain still needed to rest, so he wanted me to occasionally close my eyes and relax for a time, even when I did not feel tired.

I walked out of the hospital feeling an intense sense of victory. I started chanting one of my favourite songs, "One Life," by the Canadian band Hedley. I didn't care what anyone thought, even with my dreadful singing voice.

My brother, Mike, reflected on my journey in light of other life-changing events and losses in our family's lives.

> When my big sis sat me down and told me about the worst thing you could ever hear from her, I looked across the room at my father. I saw on his face the look I have only seen once before, when my sister Heather went through a life-changing operation herself. I completely crumbled and instantly went into denial. This could not be happening! Our hearts have been broken so many times before, and we had already lost so many people in our lives. This would not happen to my big sis.

> I hugged Lynn and, just as our little grandpa would say, she told me not to worry. Our tears stopped flowing as her confidence made us all feel so much better.

> When the operation finally happened, everyone was there for her. After months and months of so many mental and physical rollercoaster rides, Lynn pulled through. My big sister did it!

Tuesday, 30 April

Today is Shayne's 20th birthday. I've been caught up in wondering about the hereditary factor, hoping to find a plausible cause for my tumour. There is no history in my family that I have been able to verify, however Heather and I have both had benign tumours. Certainly a cause for wonder...We've tested for radon in our home and were relieved to find it well within normal ranges. I've spoken with the local Medical Officer of Health and researched the history of brain tumours in our residential area. I've sought out friends who served with me on the bridge of the training vessels when in the naval reserve. Enough is enough. It's time to accept that we will never know. What does this now mean for Shayne and his siblings? Will there need to be a screening process for them in the future? What will the research reveal as time moves forward?

Shayne was moving back from university for the summer. He had excelled in his second year, and by that time had grown into a brilliant young man who was already considering staying in school to get a PhD. He was also now the proud owner of my old Ford Escape, and he loved his freedom. It had been almost a year ago when we had first sat our children down to tell them about my diagnosis. This summer would be much different for them. Within two years, Marina and Mitch would also both be making very important decisions about their futures. I no longer feared that I wouldn't be here for them. If anything, I had the affirmation that there was nothing more important than being there to support my family.

Thursday, 15 May

My goodness, I have been remiss in writing my journal. That's what life does when it takes you over. I have learned to say "no" when I need to, and have become very adept at listening to my body. I know when I'm tired, or when I need a break or must slow down. I have increased my work schedule to four days per week. Anyone in my position who does not consider a graduated return is living in a fantasy world. I feel calmer and more confident. There have been numerous occasions where I have had to reread and relearn information. I log my task list and check it daily, and use reminders and search functions to deal with the short-term memory challenges. I am still discovering the new "me."

Marina remembers the impact those months had on her.

> My mom started healing, widening her range of speech, driving alone, and eventually returning to work. As I continue to grow as a person, I now understand how precious life truly is. I now see my mother as a role model and an inspiration. She is everything I aspire to be. As a teenager, we often fought and got on each other's nerves. We still disagree with one another, but I understand and respect her. She is caring and compassionate. I have seen her both strong and weak, but always with a smile. She is the first person I go to for advice, and she is my best friend. If she can survive a brain tumour, I can survive day by day. Everything does happen for a reason. If the reason was a lesson, it was not only for her, but for me as well. I am now so much closer to my mom.

If you or someone you love has been diagnosed with a brain tumour, the Brain Tumour Foundation of Canada has a wealth of information. They provide opportunities for both patients and caregivers to participate in online or locally-organized support groups. Their website provides numerous resources, such as newsletters and handbooks for those coping with adult, non-malignant, or paediatric brain tumours. Having facts that are reliable and grounded in research can empower us to avoid misunderstandings, to make informed decisions, and to be better prepared for the possibilities. Let's all help each other stay afloat!

Chapter Ten
Set The Sails

Thursday, 7 August

It is 12:41 in the afternoon as I write this journal entry. Twelve months ago, I was anesthetized for the craniotomy, wondering if my life was about to end. Today is very different — and it is glorious. My sister-in-law, my dear friend Susan and I went kayaking together on Grundy Lake this morning. A family of loons came so close to our kayaks that we could have reached out and touched them. Peaceful and still with the sun reflecting off the surface of the water.

Yesterday, impulsively, we deviated from our bike ride to go cliff jumping. In our clothes, we each screamed "YOLO!" as we leapt off the edge, airborne ten metres above the water. Living for the moment and laughing all the way. It is so beautiful here in the Canadian Shield: rock face, lily pads, loons, adventure and peace.

As I pore over my journal entries from that year, memories flood back. Recovery has been a long haul fraught with confusion, memory loss, reactions to medications, and a frightening period of extreme mania. It was a hurricane of exhaustion followed by over-the-top energy — a time full of bizarre mood swings, dented finger nails, hair loss, and skin rashes.

Gabriela, my neighbour, once told me that we are our own narrators. We can edit or add anything to our stories along the way. We all have things from our past that we would change if we were given the chance. Do we choose to intentionally erase experiences from our life stories? There are some experiences we share with others, and others we never will — stories full of sorrow, remorse, fear or embarrassment.

It all gives me more to ponder. "What's it all about?" "What is the purpose of this life I now lead?" I have come to the realization that the answers are moving targets. Our personal quests can only lead us to deeper understandings, which will continue to develop and change over the course of our lives.

I began by viewing this journey as a detour in my life, but it has led me to much more. There is great power in understanding that, even when there may seem to be an endless list of potential negative outcomes, we must push it all aside and focus on the positive possibilities. Our mindset affirms each moment, each day, and every small step we must take on the course to recovery — and it is important for that mindset to be a positive one.

It is also important to trust in the fact that we, as patients, always clamour with our competing treatment options, and with our personal beliefs, along the path. I liken it to long, sleepless nights of tossing and turning until we feel at peace with our own decisions.

However, we also need to recognize the power of "us" — united, together, regardless of the obstacles. The brilliance of Dr. Morassutti and the rest of the medical team has given me a future. I believe that placing confidence in their expertise, knowledge, and ability ultimately minimized my fear. Support and understanding from our loved ones can also be powerful agents of change, and can tangibly influence our recovery. I was aware that my friends and family often shielded me from their own fears and emotions, because they knew it would cause me great concern to know what they were thinking, and it would only draw my focus away from where it needed to be. In the end, however, there are no words to express how honoured and privileged I am to have each of them in my life, and how grateful I am for their support along the way. Always remember that you have an entire crew of your own to keep you afloat!

Whether you are struggling with a life-changing diagnosis yourself, or supporting a loved one through treatment for a serious condition, it is my hope that my story has equipped you, too, with new perspectives and insights.

I am a survivor with a new perspective, and I would not have it any other way. The waters are calm and the course before me is now clear.